C000246253

Words of wisdom from the Father's Heart

DAVE & JENNY GILPIN

All correspondence to:
Dave & Jenny Gilpin
Hope City Church,The Megacentre, Bernard Road, Sheffield, S2 5BQ
dave.gilpin@hopecity.co.uk
www.hopecitychurch.tv

Published by Integrity Media Europe
Unit 1 Hargreaves Business Park
Hargreaves Road, Eastbourne, BN23 6QW

ISBN 978-1-907080-05-0

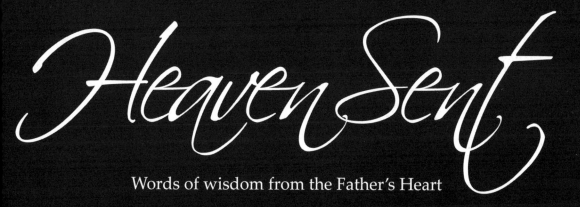

Heaven Sent

Words of wisdom from the Father's Heart

DAVE & JENNY GILPIN

aven Sent

These verses from Heaven are designed to impart God's heart, love and commitment to you and all you are becoming. Written from the perspective of your Heavenly Father this book reveals His tenderness and grace and offers a new perspective on how He speaks to us and how He leads us to a fresh encounter with His Holy Spirit. Enjoy!

Dave & Jenny Gilpin

There is nothing suspect about my timing.
I will come at just the right moment to rescue you from your place of weakness and powerlessness. Don't panic and don't lose heart. My ways are not your ways.
My timing is perfect.

"You see AT JUST THE RIGHT TIME when we were still powerless Christ died for the ungodly." *Romans 5:6 (emphasis added)*

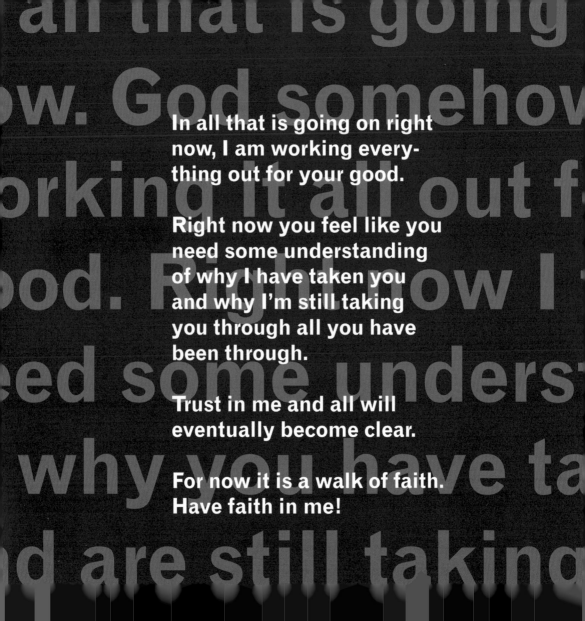

In all that is going on right now, I am working everything out for your good.

Right now you feel like you need some understanding of why I have taken you and why I'm still taking you through all you have been through.

Trust in me and all will eventually become clear.

For now it is a walk of faith. Have faith in me!

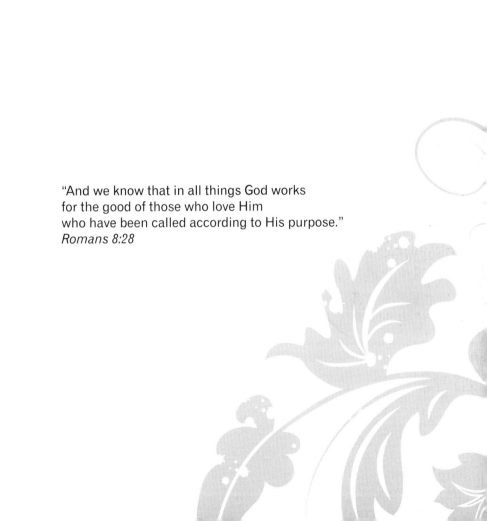

"And we know that in all things God works
for the good of those who love Him
who have been called according to His purpose."
Romans 8:28

As you simply learn to sit quietly in trust, I will fill you with all joy and peace that will lead you into an overflow of hope. I am about to give to you a fresh expectation of great things that are coming your way. But it all begins with sitting and receiving.

"May the God of hope fill you with all joy and peace as you trust in Him, so that you may overflow with hope by the power of the Holy Spirit." *Romans 15:13*

**Right now you stand in the centre of my will.
Behind the scenes of your life I am moving the furniture
in order to prepare the way for your future. I am unfolding
things in a way that you can neither see nor understand.**
DON'T MOVE A MUSCLE!
I've got it all in control.

"For My thoughts are not your thoughts. Neither are your ways My ways. As the heavens are higher than the earth, so My ways are higher than your ways and My thoughts than your thoughts." *Isaiah 55:8-9*

As you say goodbye
to your season of youth
remember your influence
and destiny is not over.
It is actually just beginning.
Allow me to expand
and break your heart
just one more time.
Everything new begins with an altar.
Follow me and I will take you deeper
into my purposes.

There is a rest I want to give you through simply knowing that you are in the centre of my will. I want you to know that what you are doing right now is just right.

Stop trying to make your life so complicated and so driven. It's time to relax in my presence, enjoy my favour and trust in me for your future.

I am an ever present help in trouble.

I'm always there - holding your hand and watching over you.

There is no need to fear even when the absolute worst is happening.

I am your refuge and strength. You will not fall.

I will keep you to the end.

This is my promise

an ever pres

"God is our refuge and strength. An ever present help in trouble. Therefore we will not fear. Even though the earth give way and the mountains fall into the heart of the sea, though its waters foam and roar and the mountains quake with their surging." *Psalm 46:1-3*

Because of my great love for you
you will not be washed away by all the pain you are feeling.
Just wait for me – it may seem like I am taking ages – but
wait for me. I will not allow it to prevail over you.
I will rescue you. I am still your Saviour.

"Yet this I call to mind and therefore I have hope. Because of the
Lord's great love we are not consumed, for His compassion never
fails. They are new every morning, great is your faithfulness. I say to
myself, the Lord is my portion, therefore I will wait for Him."
Lamentations 3:22-24

because

You may not understand the reason the why I have you in this place right now, but I am setting you up for blessing and fruitfulness. The particular requirements I am placing upon you may not make sense to you or anyone else at this time ... But once you fully understand that these requirements will take you to a higher level - a place of peace, and a new path of destiny - you will choose to follow without questioning.

"In all your ways, know, recognise and acknowledge Him and He will direct and make straight and plan your paths."
Proverbs 3:6

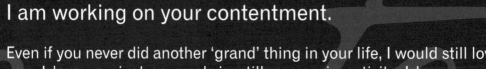

I am working on your contentment.

Even if you never did another 'grand' thing in your life, I would still love you for you. I love you just as much in stillness as in activity. I love you when you achieve great things and when you fail in great things. I love you today ... and forever more.

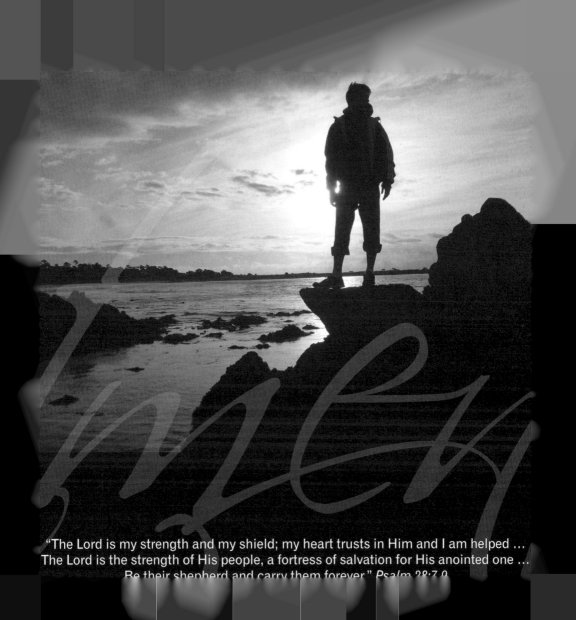

"The Lord is my strength and my shield; my heart trusts in Him and I am helped ...
The Lord is the strength of His people, a fortress of salvation for His anointed one ...
Be their shepherd and carry them forever." *Psalm 28:7-9*

IT'S TIME to acclimatise yourself again to the **Holy Spirit**. This is a season for new sensitivity and fresh acquaintance. Start to write down the dreams that I am rekindling. **Don't be shy about your dreams. I have placed them in your heart. Remember when you wrote them down years ago, and you looked back and almost all of them had come about? Do that again and watch for me. It's not as if you are chasing after them for your own advantage. These are my dreams and through your faith and followership we shall both see them come to pass. Don't ever forget that I long to bless you**

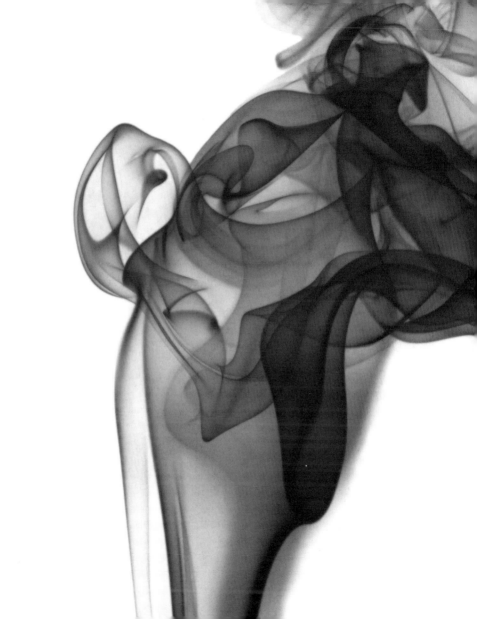

The difference between 120 and 3000*
was the outpouring of my Spirit.
I'm searching for a people who hunger
for an outpouring of my Spirit on their lives.
You'll be amazed at what I can do
when you seek me with all of your heart.

"...if my people, who are called by my name, will humble themselves and pray and seek my face and turn from their wicked ways, then will I hear from heaven and will forgive their sin and will heal their land." *2 Chronicles 7:14*

*120 people in the upper room at Pentecost came down and saw 3000 lives changed - Acts 2.

I'm ready to give

I'm ready to give you a fresh personal encounter with my Spirit – a fresh 'burning bush' experience. See how I changed Moses from an insecure runaway to a man after my heart who rescued a nation.

You may feel like Moses - all alone in the desert - but close to you is a bush that is beginning to burn. Look for it and prepare for change.

constant
forever
always
faithful & true
unfailing
ever present

Though the hills be shaken and the mountains removed – my steadfast love remains forever unshaken and my covenant remains the same. My faithfulness sits over your life. I am ever present with you. My faithfulness reaches to the heavens and touches the earth. Fear not, for I am with you!

You keep inventing where you should be and what you should do. Instead, your whole goal should be just to get to know me more. I will unravel your future. You do not need to dwell on it or stress over it. It is completely in my hands.

You cannot miss my will when you love me so much. Just run and hide under the shadow of my wings and get to know me. There are places you will go and places you will find me in that will totally delight and satisfy your soul.

There is a default switch in your heart that I need to heal. At times you seem to easily walk away from what I have called you to do. I want to heal and cleanse your heart. Let me help you to be the person and the leader I intend you to be.

Rest in me - my yoke is easy and my burden is light.

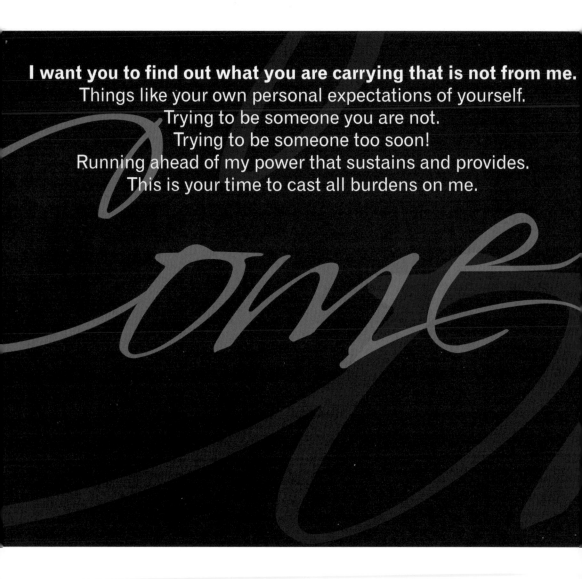

I want you to find out what you are carrying that is not from me.
Things like your own personal expectations of yourself.
Trying to be someone you are not.
Trying to be someone too soon!
Running ahead of my power that sustains and provides.
This is your time to cast all burdens on me.

"Come to Me, all you who are weary and burdened, and I will give you rest. Take My yoke upon you and learn from Me, for I am gentle and humble in heart and you will find rest for your soul. For My yoke is easy and My burden is light." *Matthew 11:28*

You called out to me...

I guide your life in completeness. I know your ways. I know your paths. I ordained you and set you apart before the beginning of time. I give you all that you need to fulfill my call for you life. Even today I am here to provide for your every need. You are my chosen vessel.

What's

...in your hand right now?

**What's in your hand will always
seem small – but don't despise it.**

**Moses began with a staff.
David began with a sling.
Mary began with a song.**

**What you have is enough.
Go in the strength that you have.**

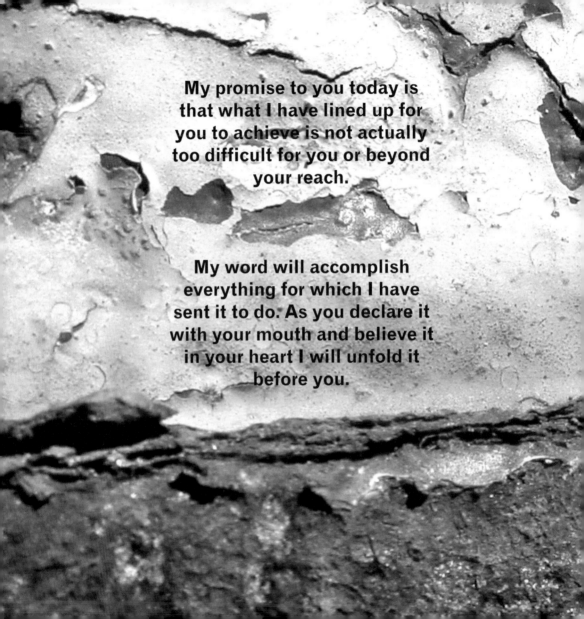

My promise to you today is
that what I have lined up for
you to achieve is not actually
too difficult for you or beyond
your reach.

My word will accomplish
everything for which I have
sent it to do. As you declare it
with your mouth and believe it
in your heart I will unfold it
before you.

"Now what I am commanding you today is not too difficult for you or beyond your reach.... No, the word is very near you; it is in your mouth and in your heart so that you may obey it."
Deuteronomy 30:11,14

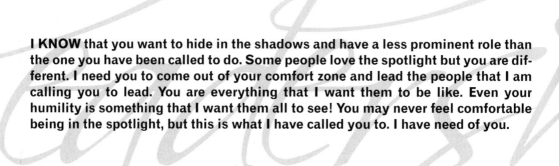

I KNOW that you want to hide in the shadows and have a less prominent role than the one you have been called to do. Some people love the spotlight but you are different. I need you to come out of your comfort zone and lead the people that I am calling you to lead. You are everything that I want them to be like. Even your humility is something that I want them all to see! You may never feel comfortable being in the spotlight, but this is what I have called you to. I have need of you.

"Today I will begin to exalt you in the eyes of all Israel, so that they may know that I am with you.... And pass on ahead of the people... And as soon as … the priests set foot …" *Joshua 3:6,7,13*

You can't earn my grace, it comes by faith and faith alone.
If you could earn it, some of my glory
would be taken away from me and placed upon you.
Everything you have ever received from me
has come from my favour and it's the same today.
Stop trying to earn what cannot be earned.
That's why it's called the favour of the Lord.

"You did not do it with your own sword and bow,
so I gave you a land on which you did not toil and cities you did not build …" *Joshua 24:12*

I am not hiding anything.
I am not keeping secrets.
I make the mysteries
of my promises known
to those who fear me.
Come closer so that I may
share them with you.

'The Lord confides in those who fear Him, He makes His covenant known to them." *Psalm 25:14*

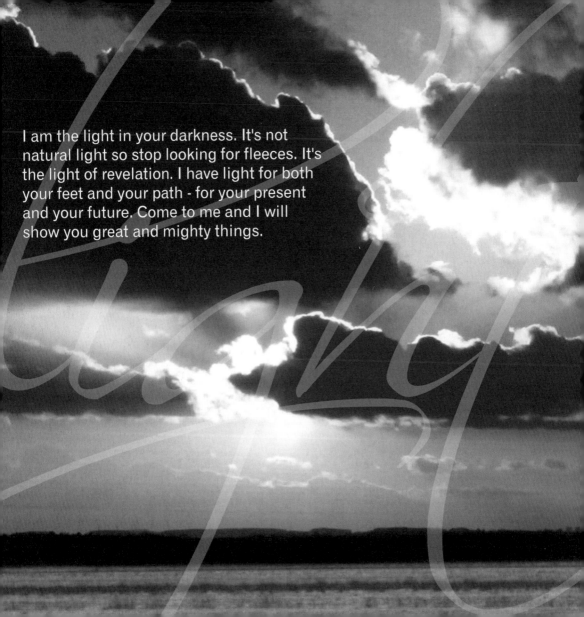

I am the light in your darkness. It's not natural light so stop looking for fleeces. It's the light of revelation. I have light for both your feet and your path - for your present and your future. Come to me and I will show you great and mighty things.

"The Lord is my light and my salvation – whom shall I fear? The Lord is the stronghold of my life – of whom shall I be afraid?" *Psalm 27:1-2*

trustworthy

**I am the most trustworthy and honest person in the universe.
I am everything that you have been looking for.**

"The man took Jesus at His word." John 4:50

Sometimes I hear you say, 'Help, I am out of my depth and in unfamiliar surroundings.' But I have brought you to this place so that I can mould you and shape you and prepare you for a new season of fruitfulness.

"My Father will honour the one who serves me. Now my heart is troubled and what shall I say? Father, save me from this hour? NO! It was for this very reason I came to this hour. Father, glorify your name!" John 12:26-27

My Spirit will speak what He hears from Me into your heart.
He will speak of My ways, My wisdom and remind you of all the
promises that I have for you today.
You are never alone. My Spirit will always be with you.

the Holy Spirit

Relax …
Be calm …
Stay anointed …
And keep listening …

"He will not speak on his own; he will speak only what he hears, and he will tell you what is yet to come. He will bring glory to me by taking from what is mine and making it known to you." *John 16:13-14*

While you have been sleeping, I have been answering.

Things have been changing and you have not been aware of it.

I never sleep and I never slumber.

I have been up all night preparing a new day and a new era for your life.

I am your Lord and your Father.

Surely my presence is with you.

GRACE

There are currently gifts of grace within you that are lying dorman
Like seeds unplanted you are full of unrealised potentia
It's time to plant your gifts into the fields that surround yo
Your harvest awaits

"But to each one of us grace has been given as apportioned it." *Ephesians*

Why are you afraid of quietness?
Do you think I go away when it is quiet?"
Remember what I have said to you -
"in quietness and trust is your strength."

hush

When you have a thankful heart and express your thankfulness to me I promise to deliver you when you call in times of trouble.

"He who sacrifices thank offerings honours me, and he prepares the way so that I may show him the salvation of God." *Psalm 50:23*

I loved you when you were just a child, without any mighty works or exploits attached. I love you the same now. I love your life even without any accompaniments. I want you to just enjoy your existence and to know that I am with you.

"One thing God has spoken, two things I have heard; that You O God are strong, and that you O Lord are loving." *Psalm 62:11-12*

"Praise be to God, who has not rejected my prayer or withheld His love from me!" *Psalm 66:20*

Every person who is looking for a great future must find a place of peace and tranquillity first. In the midst of peace my wisdom flows.

You need both new wine and new wineskins. Let me change you and clothe you in new garments. Put away the old experiences and old understanding. Start afresh with a new revelation of who I am.

"They pour new wine into new wineskins." *Matthew 9:17*

You have been living under the delusion that those who love, obey and work for me (with a right heart) are plentiful. They are not. They are scarce on the ground. That is why I need you!

"Then He said to His disciples,
the harvest is plentiful but the workers are few."
Matthew 9:37

personally

I am not far off. I am here with you, reaching out my hand to bless you. I want to fulfil my word in you and speak to you of the plans I have for your life.

My promise for you is that rivers of the Spirit shall flow from the barren heights of your life. It is on these barren heights that the cold winds of fear currently blow. You have tried to navigate and tame these mountains without success. It is in your weakness that my strength is secured and it is in your barrenness that my beauty abounds.

Don't you think I know how much goes on in your life? I am there for you.

I will anoint you, help you and be with you. I will honour the words of your mouth - the words you have spoken in faith and confidence when life had backed you into a corner with no way out except for me.

It's time to keep on declaring my promises and stepping out in obedience with all that I am saying to you.

Trust in me!

"Fear not, for I have redeemed you, I have summoned you by name; you are mine." *Isaiah 43:1*

"I have put My words in your mouth and covered you with the shadow of My hand." *Isaiah 51:16*

it's time

I come not only with salvation and righteousness, I come to you gently, riding on the unexpected – slowly, peacefully and restfully.

Gently and tenderly is how I want to speak to you. That is the way you need to relate to me. And that is how I want to relate to you.

Always remember that your life is a journey that is not accomplished over night. Through all of your ups and downs, mistakes and successes, I will gently lead you into your future. Take my hand and let's do life together.

"Rejoice greatly, O daughter of Zion! Shout daughter of Jerusalem! See your King comes to you. Righteous and having salvation. Gentle and riding on a donkey." *Zechariah 9:9*

I want to mean more to you than anything
to be your bright morning star
to meet you each morning as you wake

I am your hope
When all else fails

I am the glory and the lifter of your head
I hold your chin and tilt it upwards

I am your better future
I cleanse away your past

I am your lover
I know you completely and yet still love you

I am your destiny
You are firmly held in my hands

I AM

Be still and

"Be still and know that I am God." Psalm 46:10
"… you need only to be still." Exodus 14:14

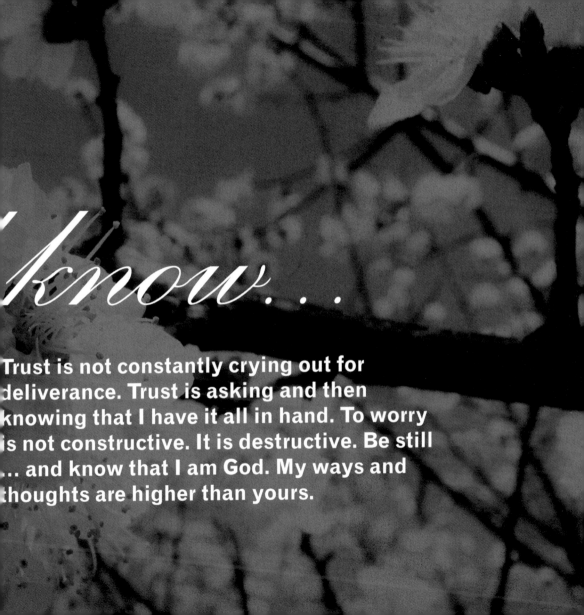

know . . .

Trust is not constantly crying out for deliverance. Trust is asking and then knowing that I have it all in hand. To worry is not constructive. It is destructive. Be still ... and know that I am God. My ways and thoughts are higher than yours.

I have set boundaries in place around your life.
Stay within the boundary lines and your life
will be pleasant and full of peace.

You are often completely unaware of my favour
and presence. Just know that I will lead you
into a place of abundance and blessing.

"The boundary lines have fallen for me in pleasant places." *Psalm 16:6*

Do not underestimate the power behind one incredible step. One step harnesses all the power of Heaven. Be aware of that. The trick is to see that I am actually behind everything in your life. That is the revelation you need. I am in every step; I give you strength, joy and peace every day. You need to just be aware of it.

The steps

The steps of a good man

I order the steps of a good man - NOT the stretches of a good man. Stop stretching. Stop trying to grab hold of an unknown future. Just be happy with steps.

Remember I am in every step.
I order them and hence there is incredible power in each one of them.

of a good man

I truly am delivering you

from all your fears. I
am bringing you to a
foundation of peace
and calmness. That
is the only basis upon
which you can walk.

I'm taking away your
fear of the future. The
wonderful thing is that
I am already in your
future. You need just to
walk into it.

I am your leader.

I am leading you beside still waters.
I am leading you into battle.
I am leading you into your future.
I am leading you into uncharted territory.

Trust and follow!

Sometimes I just want you to talk to me. Not the other way around.

Start talking - I am listening!

I am with you.
I am your personal helper.
I will defend and look after you.
Remember when you used to involve me in everything?
You think I don't want to do it anymore! I do!
Continually ask of me.

"The LORD is with me; I will not be afraid. What can man do to me? The LORD is with me; He is my helper. I will look in triumph on my enemies. It is better to take refuge in the LORD than to trust in man. It is better to take refuge in the LORD than to trust in princes." *Psalm 118:6-9*

Why have you given up dreaming?
I just want you to move
into a fresh season of favour not striving.
Let me help you to truly have a life of calmness
and also a life of anointing.

I am gently initiating you into a bigger pool.

I am slowly and gently opening a larger door into your future. If you don't respond to the door wedged slightly open, you won't be able to fulfil the rest of that which I have for your life. Just hold my hand and walk with me. Allow my light to illuminate your paths and allow my strength to hold onto you all of the way.

Commit your life into my big hands. I will look after it completely. Ask me to, and I will bless you and help you beyond your wildest dreams.

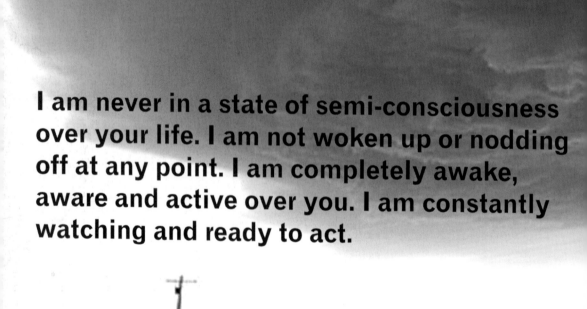

I am never in a state of semi-consciousness over your life. I am not woken up or nodding off at any point. I am completely awake, aware and active over you. I am constantly watching and ready to act.

"… for all my ways are known to you."
Psalm 119:168

"He will not let your foot slip. He who watches over you will not slumber. Indeed He who watches over Israel will neither slumber nor sleep."
Psalm 121:3-4

It is I who shade you from the intensity of your work for me, when I know it is too much for you to bear. I cover you with my wing. Hide in my presence and allow me to give you comfort.

Be aware that you are serving me. I love that about you. I love your willingness to go on loving me.

Allow me to love you.

"The Lord watches over you – the Lord is your shade at your right hand." *Psalm 121:5*

"It will be good for these servants whose master finds them watching when He comes. I tell you the truth. He will dress Himself to serve, will have them recline at the table and will come and wait on them."
Luke 12:37

There is a special reward for those who remain watchful and expectant - for those who actively expect the advancement of my Kingdom. My promise is that I will come and serve you and supply you with all that you need and all that you desire in order to fulfill my will.

Be expectant and I will move powerfully in your life. Be expectant and I will provide. Be expectant and I will bless you.

My Word

...will bud and flourish. It will achieve purpose in your life. My promises are for you as much as for everyone else.

"For My thoughts are not your thoughts. Neither are My ways your ways. As the heavens are higher than the earth, so My ways are higher than your ways and My thoughts than your thoughts." *Isaiah 55:8-9*

I know what you are going through.
I will send my Holy Spirit to you
right now to encourage your heart.

When the accuser comes, know that
you have done nothing wrong. You
are not responsible for other people's
decisions. Stay pure and stay close
to me and I will be your shield and
your advocate.

"May the Lord Jesus Christ Himself and God our Father, who loved us and by His grace
gave us eternal encouragement and good hope, encourage your hearts and strengthen
you in every good deed and word."
2 Thessalonians 3:16-17

"A bruised reed He will not break. And a smouldering wick He will not snuff out, till He leads justice to victory." *Matthew 12:20*

When you listen to my voice and what I am saying to you then you will walk with divine confidence. You will know that you are the head and not the tail. You will walk into places and carry my presence.

also available in
the **DEVOTIONAL RESCUE** series

the **DEVOTIONAL RESCUE** series

Give me mercy
Anthology of Wisdom and Inspiration

RAY BEVAN

the **DEVOTIONAL RESCUE** series

Classic Lines
Devotional Insights for Women

JENNY GILPIN

the **DEVOTIONAL RESCUE** series

IT'S TIME TO LEAVE THE
Cemetery

REPOSITIONING YOUR LIFE FOR THE NEXT BIG THING!
RAY BEVAN